All Scripture references taken from the KJV of the Holy Bible, unless otherwise indicated.

Fruit of the Womb: Prayers Against Barrenness *Book 2*, by Dr. Marlene Miles

Freshwater Press, USA

ISBN: 978-1-960150-84-4

Paperback Version

Copyright 2023 by Dr. Marlene Miles

All rights reserved. No part of this book may be reproduced, distributed, or transmitted by any means or in any means including photocopying, recording or other electronic or mechanical methods without prior written permission of the publisher except in the case of brief publications or critical reviews.

Table of Contents

A Fruitful Womb 4
God's Order: Get Married First 13
The One You Want to Marry 18
Lord, Deal Bountifully with Me 22
Heal the Foundation 29
Your Mouth, Your Unbelief 36
Goodbye Spirit "*Relatives*" 43
Prayer for a Child 46
Unrighteous Seed 49
Warfare *to* the Womb 56
Warfare *In* the Womb 63
Delivery Warfare 69
Keep Praying for Your Child 73
Pregnancy Dreams 81
Prayer for Righteous Seed 85
Children Get Along Together 90
Finances 91
Hannah's Celebration 93
Acknowledgements 96
Christian books by this author 97

Fruit of the Womb
Prayers Against Barrenness
Book 2

Dear Reader:

Thank you for reading this book and supporting this ministry. God's grace and blessings on your life and bloodline, in the Name of Jesus.

Amen.

Dr. Marlene Miles

Freshwater Press, USA

A Fruitful Womb

God created for six days before conditions were right to bring forth man. In God's image we do what He does, the way He does it. It may take considerable awareness and preparation before the conditions are right to bring forth righteous seed. Then, like God, you too can rest from *creating*.

A lot of women and couples delay having children. I have given birth to no children, not for having tried. In that, don't be like me.

I did not freeze my eggs because I didn't think it was necessary, and as it was not as common when I was in my 20's and 30's as it has become these days. It is, however, very expensive; data states that about 80% of women conceive with their own frozen ova. That option takes faith, but the other option, to not freeze the eggs like Sarah, Abraham's wife, takes even more faith. For a barren woman, conceiving, carrying and giving birth especially to your first child may take the *most* faith.

> **Sing, O barren**, thou that didst not bear; break forth into singing, and cry aloud, thou that didst not travail with child: for more are the children of the desolate than the children of the married wife, saith the Lord. (Isaiah 54:1)

A woman tried for years to become a mother, in multiple marriages. She thought each marriage was of God and that the men were Christian men.

The first husband was impotent; could not get or maintain an erection. He professed being a Christian, although they went to church only once during their courtship. But he did not want pre-marital sex, which pleased her; but there was no way for the woman to know of his impotence before the marriage night. Actually, there was no sex on the marriage night, **he** was *"too tired."* If he ever went for treatment for this ED, she never knew it. If she were wiser, she would have seen how much he drank in his past and known what devastation alcoholism can do to a man's reproductive performance and virility. This husband was asked what was his stress as to why he couldn't get an erection or maintain one--, what was on his mind? He said to become and remain aroused he just thought of all kinds of sexual thoughts?

Such as?

People, things he's seen, and so on, was his reply. What in the world has he *seen*, she wondered.

This man was conjuring up demons. I hate to start this book out talking about *spirit spouse*, but this man's imagination was calling up *spirit spouse* whether he knew it or not. Spirit spouse is opposed to marriage, because it thinks it is already married to you; it is jealous and sometimes violently so. Spirit spouse is on assignment against humans having natural children. If *spirit spouse* is present, then spirit children are also already present.

In intimate encounters, if you are not with your spouse and your *mind* is not on that spouse, you are inviting all kinds of stuff into the bedroom. You should be married to one spouse and having relations with that one spouse, after having prayed before relations, every single time, to bring forth and bring forth Godly seed.

What's your fantasy? No! That should never be a question or entertained in a Christian marriage. Sorry. Fantasies are soulish. Soulish prayers invite the devil.

This woman's second husband also was a professed Christian, but didn't shy away from the sex act, premaritally, even without **her** consent. As a devout Christian, she told him *goes into* equals married, so he had to marry her. They got married.

Folks like to sample the wares, but premarital sex can set a couple up for difficulty in conception because of the *iniquity* that goes along with the sin.

Fornication is sin.

As we learned from the first book in this series, sin has many consequences and one of them is barrenness. Shortly after they were married, the second husband confessed that he had, in his words, *"paltry semen."* Whether he meant a low ejaculate volume, or a low sperm count, or both, it wasn't clear.

Later on, she found out that Husband #2 loved pornography. While in bed together, he would watch pornography after he thought she was asleep. He did not realize that she could see what he was watching through the mirror on the dresser in their bedroom opposite the TV. After watching this trash, he would try to wake her up to *finish*. She would pretend to not wake up, until one night she couldn't take it anymore, she "woke up," and told him to *finish* the way he started. That was the end of that. Don't be like that man.

No children were born of that marriage, either.

Pornography creates soul ties with every person in the video--, male or female, doesn't matter. You're married to them.

Spirit spouse again. It's why the Bible says to not spy out another's liberties – that means, you don't look on their nakedness. There is Old Testament record of folks who got into trouble for "uncovering nakedness." Pornography stimulates lustful, fantasy imagination, inviting **demons** that will call themselves *spirit spouse--*, anti-conception spirit spouse. Don't be like those people.

Pray. I reverse all damage to my body and life as a result of defilement by unauthorized and unconventional intercourse, in Jesus' Name. *Amen.*

There was a third husband, who had a child already, so his plumbing obviously worked. This wife had been to multiple doctors over the years and was told that there was no reason why she couldn't conceive. One day the woman came home to see her new husband laying on the couch with an ice pack over his groin area. She ran to him, *Honey, what happened, are you okay?*

He said, "I had a procedure today."

"What procedure?"

His answer was like a heavy anvil hitting the floor, *"Today I got a vasectomy."*

You got a what!

He continued the argument that he had started, *"I don't want any more children."*

Wow, she thought, it was not as if they were really having relations all that often anyway--, but wow! That was the end of the third marriage--, six months.

How could one woman encounter this many issues related to conception, yet be fertile herself? Evil foundation? Was ba*rrenness* in her foundation, so she attracted three different versions of the same problem? No, all other family members were very fertile. Evil dedication? Was she dedicated to some evil unawares? Evil exchange? Witchcraft? Y

Don't be like that woman. Pray to God before marriage to know about yourself and what you're dealing with.

As a Christian, when you marry, you may not know some of the things that this woman suffered because talking about sex is often taboo. Sometimes that lack of *real talk* about sex transfers into the marriage itself and neither party open up. Here are some real questions to ask; and get your answers.

1. Do you *want* to get married?
2. Do you want to *be* married?
3. Do you want to **stay** married?
4. Do you want to have children?
5. How many children?
6. How do you want to raise them?
7. Are you from a polygamous background? That's a nice way of asking, *What's your body count?* Every non-virgin is polygamous. Period. If their daddy was a rolling stone, polygamy is in the DNA, unless deliverance has taken place.
8. As far as you know are you fertile, or at least non-sterile?
9. Last check up?
10. History of diseases of any kind? Family and personal.
11. Do you have a normal sperm count?
12. Do you have regular cycles? Any history of infertility in your family?

Pray

Lord, I repent for every personal sin which has brought on the Curse of the Law, which *barrenness* is a part. Lord, hear my repentance, forgive me and remove the curse of barrenness from me, in Jesus' Name.

Every power fighting my success and destiny, catch Fire now, in Jesus' Name.

Every altar working against my marriage, catch Fire now, in Jesus' Name.

Powers from my mother's or father's side allowing barrenness in my marriage, body, or life, be rooted out now, and cast to the bottomless pit, in Jesus' Name.

Spirit of barrenness, I cast you out of my life and the life of my spouse, in Jesus' Name.

I apply the Blood of Jesus to my spirit, soul, body, and reproductive organs, now, in the Name of Jesus.

Any name or label placed on me that does not allow my Star to shine, be erased now by the power in the Blood of Jesus.

God's Order: Get Married First

Years ago, when I was 25 or so, a 15-year-old asked me how many children I had. I told her, *None.* She asked me what was wrong with me. I told her, *"Nothing, I'm not married. I need to get married and have a husband first.* She had no idea what I was talking about. All things should be done decently and in order, but in the world in which she lived having a baby was for reasons other than bringing Godly seed to the Earth. Not finding anyone or the right one to marry may mean that you are under the Curse of the Law.

Lord, forgive me for anything that would stand against my prayers, in the Name of Jesus.

Lord, none of us are perfect, but send me a spouse who will disclose **everything** that needs to be disclosed to have a successful relationship and marriage and give me Grace and Wisdom to handle what I hear, in the Name of Jesus.

Lord, search me, deliver me, heal me; make me a Kingdom spouse candidate. Send me my Kingdom spouse, in the Name of Jesus.

Lord, send a spouse who will disclose any medical, physical, emotional and *spiritual* issues that need to be dealt with **before** marriage so it will be well with us, and we can have a successful marriage and family, in the Name of Jesus.

I cancel every bewitchment against my getting married, staying married and being happy in marriage, in the Name of Jesus.

I reject every anti-marriage spell against me, in the Name of Jesus.

I cancel every ancestral curse against my getting married, staying married and being happy in marriage, from both sides of my family, in the Name of Jesus.

If married, you can pray the above also for your spouse. If not married, your intended must pray the above. It would be best that the two of you pray *together* and seek deliverance if possible. Premarital counseling, in my opinion should include deliverance.

Pray

Lord, let every force bringing the wrong people into my life be paralyzed, in the Name of Jesus.

I command all forces of evil delay or hinderance to my marriage to be bound and completely paralyzed, in Jesus' Name.

I break every evil covenant of marital failure and late marriage, including my own soul ties and evil foundation, in the Name of Jesus.

Let all evil anti-marriage marks placed on me or my life be removed by the Blood of Jesus, in Jesus' Name.

I cancel every spiritual wedding involving me, with or without my knowledge, in the Name of Jesus.

Childhood weddings, Tom Thumb, et cetera, childhood betrothments and pledges that parents hoped would turn into real marriages, or just thought were cute, be canceled now: I issue a writ of divorce, in the Name of Jesus.

Plays and dramatizations of marriages that I participated in, I cancel you all, in Jesus' Name.

Childhood marriage and wedding day fantasies, childhood crushes, and *pretend* marriages, be canceled now, in the Name of Jesus.

I divorce every person or actor that ever stood up with me, beside me in any play, movie, skit, or enactment, in Jesus' Name.

Lord, restore me to the perfect way You created me to be; restore my soul, in the Name of Jesus. Make me single and **whole** and ready to be in a Kingdom marriage.

(If already married, pray) Lord, make our marriage a Kingdom marriage, in Jesus' Name.

Lord, expose all enemy schemes against me and my marriage; Holy Spirit, give me what and how to pray about it, in Jesus' Name.

Lord, please forgive, and I also forgive my parents and ancestors for evil dedication whether they were tricked, duped, ignorant, or greedy. Please release me from all evil dedication, in Jesus' Name.

Lord forgive me for all personal sin that has given ground to the enemy, especially sexual sin, in the Name of Jesus.

I break all satanic connections and any linkage to *strange* people, in the Name of Jesus.

Lord, I know You will bless a well-ordered person, a well-ordered marriage, a well-ordered family with well-mannered children; let that be the case for me and mine, in the Name of Jesus. *Amen.*

The One You Want to Marry

Is the one you want to marry fruitful, productive marriage material? Husband or wife *material*? Parent material?

Ask God what their status is. The Lord was dealing with me, just last night. We went over the inventory of my former love interests, dates, suitors, and husbands. I am a woman, so the Holy Spirit took me over the status of their *seed*.

He told me which ones were acceptable to Him, seed wise, and which ones whose seed He *had cut off*. Had I asked those questions years ago, during the courtships, I would have been far better off. I tell you now so you will do just that. When you want to present your person to God to see what God says, God doesn't look on the outside, how tall, how short, long hair, red hair, brown hair--, God looks on the inside, at the heart. Most people when describing their perfect mate will describe physical attributes and little to nothing more. That's not even what God is looking at.

More than that, God already **knows** your person, this is not the first time God has met or learned about your person's existence.

God and this person already have a *relationship*, good or bad, they already have a relationship. God made the Heavens and the Earth. God breathed into each of us to make us living souls; He knows who is here, when they got here *and* what they have been doing the whole time they've been here. Nobody is not under God's watchful eye.

A person who is not saved is not just not saved; they don't just have a neutral, unknown relationship with God; **they have a BAD relationship with God.**

Until that bad relationship situation is rectified, this should not be someone that you want to marry, or allow them to provide ½ of the DNA of your offspring, and be the *other* parent of your children. All the stuff you see in this unsaved, or saved and carnal mate, and may cringe at, will be in your children and in their lives. All the stuff that you don't see that will take you by surprise will also be in your little ones.

I remove the right of the enemy to block me from getting married, by the power in the Blood of Jesus.

Angels of the Only Living God, remove every blockage to my Kingdom marriage, in the Name of Jesus.

All masquerading *spirits* troubling my marital life be bound, in the Name of Jesus.

I receive my Kingdom match, in the Name of Jesus. Thank You, Lord.

Lord, turn away all that will jilt, disappoint or fail me; do not let me marry **the assignment of the devil,** in Jesus' Name.

Lord, send me a spouse that will not neglect the family prayer altar, in Jesus' Name.

Divine Axe of God, cut down all our foundation problems at their roots, in the Name of Jesus.

Father God, pull down every stronghold up against me, in the Name of Jesus.

Holy Spirit redirect every evil wind sent against my home and marriage; back to sender, in the Name of Jesus.

Lord, go ahead of every potential problem that could result from a second, third or *any* marriage, in the Name of Jesus.

All witchcraft *spirits* monitoring my marital situation, be blinded now by the power of the Holy Spirit, in Jesus' Name. *Amen.*

Lord, Deal Bountifully with Me

Now you're married to a wonderful spouse and you two are walking in step and side by side. Two cannot walk together unless they agree (Amos 3:3). You both have agreed that it is time to have a child and you've begun to *"try."* You trust each other and definitely want to have a child together. Do you two purpose to stay married and raise your child together and build a life together? Those questions need to be asked and answered. Parenting as a single is not impossible, but it is difficult and it is neither God's plan, nor His best for the single parent, or the child.

Pray────── Lord, deal bountifully with me, and open my womb, in the Name of Jesus. *Amen.*

Jehovah Sabaoth

If you are not pregnant within a year of *trying*, spiritual warfare and or deliverance may be required.

In 1 Samuel 1:3 Hannah cries out to God for a son. **That is warfare** not just because of the reproach and the shame of barrenness, but because of the intensity of the *accusations* and torment hurled at Hannah, who had no child. It was warfare because she was tormented by her human persecutor, her sister-wife, Peninnah for having no child and specifically, *no son*. It doesn't say so in the Bible, but how do we know what any sister-wife is doing to another to keep her from becoming pregnant? Competition in polygamy is tremendous. Especially those who say what they are going to do to you or fling a lot of torment your way, sometimes they are complicit; witchcraft, especially in polygamy, abounds.

Hannah answered her tormentor by intense prayers--, warfare prayers to God.

When we war as we are supposed to, we are made *sons* of God, Mighty warriors. When we are sons of God then we also war spiritually; that's not all we do, but that is a part of *sonship*. Hannah had no son and before His only begotten Son, God also had no sons in the sense that Jesus was the *firstborn of many brethren*.

The devil stands at the Throne of God, day and night accusing the brethren. Surely you've felt shame and reproach as if something is wrong with you. There may be nothing wrong with you that is not common to man; it is that you feel that *spirit of accusation*. Day and night.

God also wanted sons. He wanted children--, sons that he could be proud of and well pleased about. God said in Genesis, **Be fruitful and multiply**, and that's why, I believe, He also heard Hannah's prayers.

God wanted to be fruitful and multiply, as well. Hannah's prayer was 100% Scriptural. Make sure your prayers are Scriptural and God will hear and answer them.

> ***Thou art my beloved Son, in Whom I am well pleased.*** (Psalm 2:7)
>
> God knew them in advance and He decided in advance that we would be conformed to the image of His son. (Romans 8:29)

As far as we know the women of the Bible who cried out to God for children and to have their wombs *"opened"* were virgins when they met their husbands and had no soul ties to other men. Unless relationship issues came down their bloodline through iniquity, they had no curses on them as to why they didn't conceive. We don't know if they had *spirit spouse* or not, but fallen angels have been sleeping with the daughters of men since Genesis 6:6. We will believe these women did not, but we don't know anything about the sexual history of the men of "barren women." But because these women didn't have children, whatever their conception problems were, they had to be delivered from them to conceive. Those problems could have been any and all of the above, plus inherited stuff.

The woman is often accused of being the reason why she is **not** pregnant, but the man must be fertile and functioning, as well. Actually, the woman is to blame if she *is* pregnant in an unwanted pregnancy—more *spirit of accusation*. Adam started this habit of accusing Eve for the sin in which he also participated.

A barren wife might be the result of a **sterile (barren)** husband who is not able to impregnate her. However, in Bible days there were no OB's to tell her that her reproductive health was fine and no urologists to tell him that his sexual and reproductive health wasn't. Their faulty belief, therefore, was that it was *her* fault.

Infertility is warfare, best fought by the husband and the wife together. One can put a thousand to flight, and two can put 10,000 to flight. Together. Delayed conception or other fertility issues is not the time to fight one another. The warfare is not against humans, and certainly not against your spouse.

Hannah cried out and Jehovah Sabaoth arose because of her prayers. God will move Heaven and Earth for just **one**. *Are you that one?* Cry out to God; He will show up for you as well. This is warfare. If you are His *son*, he will do it for you. Remember, there is no gender in God, so a *son*, to God, is male **or** female. When God created the man and then the woman, He called both of them Adam. Adam, who was given authority to name everything; named the woman, Eve.

Jehovah Sabaoth is a Mighty Warrior. Who is obstructing your being fruitful and multiplying? Then that is an enemy of God and your enemy, as well. It's not *you*, is it? If you are self-sabotaging, or obstructing God, that is your first repentance, if the weapon that has been formed against you was created, allowed, or inside of you--, repent!

Now that we know it's not you, we must battle, we must war. God's Word will perform, and God's power is absolute. We war not against flesh and blood. Hannah didn't beef with her husband, Elkanah, nor even the sniveling, Peninnah. She took it to the Spirit; she took her issue, that battle, to God, our Mighty Warrior, in prayer.

Jesus came from Heaven to Earth because of the war. Yes, the war for men's souls, but also the personal wars that anyone in Christ would face in this life. Count it not strange that these things have come upon you. God is teaching your hands to war and your fingers to fight. He expects you to be victorious as a *son*. Win this war and your kingship will be assured. Kings in the Bible were warriors.

Pray

Lord, get me out of the way of Your deliverance for me, in Jesus' Name. *Amen*

Heal the Foundation

Your child will inherit the spiritual foundation that the other parent is carrying as well as yours. Sure, your beloved looks good, cute and attractive, but what do you know of them *spiritually*? What do you know of their foundation?

What do you know of your own foundation, for that matter? All the ways of a man are clean in his own eyes, but you've got to be real, now. You won't change the proclivities in your child by any natural thing you do. Not by giving them everything they want, making them *happy*, wishing the best for them every day, and making sure they do all the stuff you wanted to do as a child, or all the stuff that is considered *cool*. Nope, that won't change <u>foundation.</u> Foundation is spiritual.

You can change the paint on the walls of your house every month, but an unchanged foundation remains the same. You have got to deal with what is in your child's foundation, in **both** bloodlines – mother's and father's. The possibilities can be exhausting.

Don't compromise. Your future spouse's family is well off, but let's say they are criminals. You may say, *At least I'll be financially comfortable.* Please THINK about what you are doing here.

Lord, make me mindful that the foundation I was born into greatly affects my life, the life of my spouse, and ultimately the life of our child. Deliver us, O Lord, in Jesus' Name.

I cover myself with the Blood of Jesus. Lord release me from inherited iniquity, and bondage, in the Name of Jesus.

Lord, thank You that I can be delivered from any bondage; nothing is too hard for You, in the Name of Jesus.

Lord, I confess my sins and sins of my ancestors, especially those linked to evil powers.

I vomit every evil consumption that I have been fed from a baby to now, in the Name of Jesus.

I command all foundational strongmen attached to my life to be paralyzed, in the Name of Jesus.

I break every inherited evil covenant, in Jesus' Name.

I break every inherited evil curse, in the Name of Jesus.

Father, break the curse and sequela of polygamy off my family and household, in the Name of Jesus.

Let every gate opened by evil to my foundation be closed forever with the Blood of Jesus.

Lord, Jesus, from my birth to now, deliver me, heal me and make me over in Your image and likeness, in the Name of Jesus; make me a *son*.

I reject, revoke, and renounce any membership in any evil association, cult, or secret society, in the Name of Jesus.

I break all evil covenants I have entered into knowingly, or not, in the Name of Jesus.

I bind every demon attached to every evil covenant and cast them into the deep, in the Name of Jesus.

I resist every invocation to draw me backward or to return to any evil association, with the Blood of Jesus, in Jesus' Name.

Holy Spirit, build a wall of Fire around me that will make it impossible for any *evil spirit* to come *at* me again, in Jesus' Name.

Lord, break down the evil foundation of my life and rebuild it with Christ the Solid Rock.

I break every curse placed on me by my parents, or any relatives, inadvertently or on purpose, in the Name of Jesus.

I break every curse, spell, hex, enchantment, bewitching, incantation placed on me by any satanic agent. Lord, forgive me that any curse was ever able to alight on me, in Jesus' Name.

Father Lord, let my deliverance be permanent, do not let these same enemies capture me again, in the Name of Jesus.

I break myself loose from every collective covenant, in the Name of Jesus.

I break every evil covenant with idols and the yoke attached to it, in the Name of Jesus.

Confusion, go into the camp of all evil agents plotting against my progress, in the Name of Jesus.

I break every evil covenant and it's curse entered into by my parents on my behalf and all the bondages and yokes attached to it. I bind every enforcing demon of any curse, in the Name of Jesus.

Lord, make my paths confusing to the enemy, in the Name of Jesus.

Let all the adversaries of my breakthrough be put to shame, in the Name of Jesus.

Lord, you have the power to deliver me from every yoke and bondage, in Jesus' Name.

I renounce and loose myself from every evil dedication placed on my life, in Jesus' Name.

I command all demons associated with evil dedication to leave now. I take authority over all curses associated with any evil dedication, in Jesus' Name.

Lord, cancel the evil consequences of any broken demonic promise or dedication, in Jesus' Name.

I take authority over all curses emanating from breaking dedication vows, in the Name of Jesus.

Lord, heal and reverse all the damage done, to my life and body, in the Name of Jesus.

I reject every *spirit of doubt, fear* and *discouragement,* in the Name of Jesus.

Lord, separate me completely from all the sins of my forefathers by the precious Blood of Jesus.

Lord, hear my repentance, Lord – please remove the curse, if it is from You.

O Lord, let Your Word perform in my life.

O Lord, avenge me of my adversaries.

God of Elijah who answers by Fire, answer me by Fire, in the Name of Jesus.

God who quickens the dead, quicken my womb, quicken my manhood, in the Name of Jesus.

God who calls those things that be not as if they were, answer me by Fire; call me fertile, in the Name of Jesus.

I vomit out every satanic deposit in my life, in the Mighty Name of Jesus Christ.

Lord, destroy with your Fire anything that makes Your promise fail in my life, in Jesus' Name.

Your Mouth, Your Unbelief

To anyone who may have been unsaved and *in the world,* in sin, but now saved and trying to conceive, seeing your *monthly* every month is emotionally painful and tormenting, when it used to be the most welcome thing when you were in sin, and in the world. You must be saved, renounce the world and accept Jesus Christ as your Lord and Savior, and never look back, except to repent.

You must break your covenant with the world. That covenant that you unwittingly made when you begged every month for your cycle to start--, *Please start, please start.* By that prayer, an agreement was made with *Molech* and/or *Herodian spirits* that hate and kill children.

You begged because as long as your cycle started you thought you got away with what you had done the previous days of that 28-day cycle.

Worse than just praying and saying it, you meditated on it, maybe obsessed on it. If you were waiting for your time of the month you thought about it every waking moment. That is meditation. No, you don't have to sit in a circle, cross-legged, with your eyes closed to meditate. Just keeping the same thought, things, words on your mind for any length of time, but especially all day long, is meditating. Oh, if you would meditate on the Word of God and the promises of God like that now.

You had faith for it too. You did not leave home without everything you needed *just in case*.

Have that kind of faith in God.

At that time, you were in the world and may not have realized that everything you did, whether you got "caught" in the natural world, was recorded in the spiritual world. So, you really got away with nothing. Your words and actions put a lot of things in motion that need to be taken out of motion for your life to proceed in a Godly fashion now that you're saved.

If you are having a hard time in any area of your life now, that may be evidence of what I'm saying here. Let's change that *please start* prayer to **PLEASE REPENT**.

Seriously, the *please start* prayer resounds, until you stop it. Prayer transcends space and time; that prayer is echoing in the Spirit, in the heavenlies. Any prayer that you pray that is **ungodly** is a soulish prayer, and it will not be answered by God, but by the devil and it creates a soul tie, an evil initiation, and an evil covenant. All of those things must be broken.

It's complicated. But in this book, we will work diligently to sort all this out.

Evil vows that I have spoken, in jest or that others have led me to speak, thinking it's funny, I renounce them all, in Jesus' Name.

I renounce and revoke all the oaths I took knowingly or not while entering any evil association or secret society, in Jesus' Name.

Blood of Jesus, cry me out of every, *I will love you forever* vow I've made with or spoken to anyone who is not my Kingdom spouse, in the Name of Jesus.

Lord, deliver me from all the word curses that I have spoken out of my own mouth, in the Name of Jesus.

To die for? **Nothing is to die for**. Lord, forgive me, I renounce and denounce those evil words in Jesus' Name.

Forgive me for all the times I said anti-life or fruitless words over my own body, life, marriage, children, job, or business, in the Name of Jesus.

Lord, bring to my recall and forgive me of every secular SONG of unbelief I have ever sung that joined me with the kingdom of darkness and is now blocking my life in any way, especially my fertility, in Jesus' Name.

I will **NOT** give my first born to any human or evil agent, for any reason, ever, in the Name of Jesus.

Lord, I renounce ever having spoken words that relinquish body parts--, left arm, right leg, et cetera, in exchange for **anything**.

Lord, I renounce ever saying or implying the *signing of my life away* for anything, ever, in the Name of Jesus.

I renounce ever saying, *I would do anything for* _____, in the Name of Jesus.

I cancel, by the Blood of Jesus every evil covenant created because of ignorant words, evil words, clichés and ridiculous sayings that I have spoken that have given license to the devil in my life.

Lord, cancel any words that I have ever spoken in spite, hatred, resentment, or bitterness over my own productivity and success in life, in Jesus' Name.

I bind and paralyze every demon sent to enforce the evil covenants made by those ignorant and evil vows and oaths, in the Name of Jesus.

I cancel the consequences of any evil name given to me purposefully, or in ignorance, in the Name of Jesus.

Let all wickedness rising up against my marriage, fertility, life, and family, be made impotent, whether they are standing on my evil vow or not, in the Name of Jesus.

I blot out every evil mark, incision, or writing placed in my spirit and body as a result of my membership in any evil association, in the Name of Jesus.

I withdraw any part of my body and body fluids at any evil altar, because I uttered an evil vow, in the Name of Jesus.

I withdraw my name, picture, image, and spirit from every evil altar, in Jesus' Name.

I withdraw my name, permanently from every evil register by the power in the Blood of Jesus.

Fire of God, roast to ashes every evil bird, snake, or other animal attached to my life, in any way, by any means. Any serpent sent to bite me, miss your mark, bite your sender, then yourself and die, in Jesus' Name.

I return all artifacts of evil associations I am connected to, in any way, I rid myself and my home of all items belonging to idol *gods* in my possession, in the Name of Jesus.

All doors of blessings and breakthrough shut against me by any evil association, I command you to be opened, in Jesus' Name.

I purge myself of all the evil foods I have eaten in the dream or in my awake life by the Blood of Jesus.

I break and revoke every blood and soul tie covenant and attached yokes and bondages to any satanic agent, in the Name of Jesus.

All *scorpion spirits* sent against me, lose your sting against me; sting your sender, then yourself and die, in the Name of Jesus.

Goodbye Spirit "*Relatives*"

Spirit spouse interferes with and blocks marriages, conception, and having natural children. You and your spouse could each have one or more *spirit spouses*. Spirit spouses make couples fight. *His* spirit spouse tells him everything that is wrong with her and how he can do better. *Her* spirit spouse tells her how horrible he is and how he can't be trusted, and she deserves better. Demons are having a field day; do not be their victim.

They fight. If they can't see through the devil's tactics, they don't make love, they fight. All *spirit spouses* need to be divorced.

I break every covenant with any sex demon, especially from the evil water kingdom.

Water *spirits* that trouble my dream life, die, in the Name of Jesus.

I bind and paralyze every astral projecting power from entering my home, bed, or *me*, in the Name of Jesus.

I bind and eject the *spirit of the dog* from my soul, spirit and body, in Jesus' Name.

Lord, send a wall of fire, and ministering angels all around me, in the Name of Jesus.

I bind and paralyze every anti-pregnancy *spirit*, in the Name of Jesus.

I renounce, break and loose myself from all demonic holds, psychic powers, and every bondage, by the Blood of Jesus.

Spirit spouse of every kind, my body is the temple of the Holy Spirit, redeemed, cleansed, sanctified, set aside, in Jesus' Name.

All *spirits* attached to pornography, come out of me, come out of my womb, out of my reproductive organs, with all your roots, in Jesus' Name.

Get out, *spirit spouse*, in the Name of Jesus.

Every marriage in the spirit realm blocking or interfering with my real marriage in the physical, scatter and die, in Jesus' Name.

Get lost, *spirit children*; I don't want you, you are not welcome in my life, in the Name of Jesus.

Spirit spouse, of any origin, I terminate your access to my dream and physical life; no more access to me, in Jesus' Name.

The power that does not belong in my bed but is in love with my bed, let my bed become Fire, in the Name of Jesus.

My whole bed is the Blood of Jesus.

Whatever I have been doing that gives invitation or power to *spirit spouse*, I stop it now, I renounce it, I denounce it, in Jesus's Name; Lord, forgive me.

Prayer for a Child

I asked a woman who had believed for many years, and then, finally conceived, after her child had become a tormenting teenager what had she prayed to God for back when she was asking for a child. She answered that she just prayed for a child--, any child.

If God is desirous of bringing righteous seed to the Earth, find out exactly what that is and pray for that, line by line. Do not leave to chance what you may get; that is the same as giving up. Don't ever give up.

Most parents will answer the gender question with, *As long as it is healthy.* That's good, but that's too general. Hannah's vow was that her son would be dedicated to God, that meant Hannah was doubling down on being fruitful and bringing righteous seed to the Earth, so much so that her seed would be dedicated to God from birth, and Samuel was. Hannah fulfilled her vow.

More importantly, righteous seed is not a what, or an *it*, it is a **who**. Pray for **PURPOSE** and spiritual gifts in your child, even before you ever conceive them. Describe that child to God; He will hear you.

Who is God sending to Earth through you? If you don't know, then how will you bring them up properly? How will you train them up in the way that they should go? You should not have to accept a hardheaded, foolish, or rebellious child, but Godly seed of good nature and good temperament who will hear God and obey God from an early age. A child like Hannah's Samuel, could be your child. Ask God that your child will be great and do exploits in His Name.

Be honest with God; He knows your heart anyway. **WHY** do you want a child. To *say* you have one? Because your friends have one? Because grandma keeps asking you? Just to experience it? Because they are cute, and you can post their pictures online? To make *you* look good? To make you feel important? To tie your spouse down? To be your best friend? Because they are fun? Whatever your reason, find precedent in the Bible and stand on it. None of the aforementioned are reasons to have a child, biblically.

Every power fighting my fruitfulness, catch Fire. Anti fruitfulness powers from my mother's or father's side be rooted out now, and cast into the pit, in Jesus' Name.

Lord, I pray against unfriendly friends, evil relatives, and/or stealth enemies up against me, my marriage, my spouse, or my child.

I pray against demonic initiation by the evil laying on of hands, tainted natural or *spirit* food, by the Blood of Jesus.

Lord, give us our child's name; do not let us misname our child, in the Name of Jesus.

Lord, tell me our child's *calling* and spiritual gifts, so we will know how to raise him.

Unrighteous Seed

You ask God for Godly things. Everything ungodly that you ask for, if it is being answered, it's not God who is answering; it is the devil. Get the devil out of your womb by asking for a Godly child and dedicating your child to God.

Yes, you want a child or maybe more than one. But you don't want to throw your seed and your womb out there for just anyone to use. The devil wants to bring more evil human agents into the Earth, recruit them from birth, get at them in the womb, have an evil or ignorant parent dedicate them to Satan, the world, or initiate them as soon as possible.

Do not have babies for Babylon. Be very clear and specific as to what your desires are to God so you do not bring forth Rosemary's baby or unrighteous seed of any kind. If your child is not dedicated to God, God's protection against them being captured by the devil is limited.

I'm sure that I'm not talking about you, but could this be the struggle? God knows what you would do with, or to a child or how you will bring them up.

Surely, you've noticed people who should do better seem to pop out children all the time; those are children of the flesh. They which are the children of the flesh, these are not the children of God, (Romans 9:8a). God wants to bring righteous seed to the Earth. All the wombs that were closed in the Bible that God later "opened" brought forth righteous seed. God slowed things down long enough to make the parents aware and for the **parents to get in position to have and rear a child of promise.**

Can you be the one? We bind up every snail spirit, every delay, unless the delay slows us down for God's purposes.

Show God that you are serious and righteous and trying to live in holiness and you will bring your child up that way without being overbearing and turning your child away from God. But the children of the promise are counted for the seed, (Romans 9:8b)

Keep in mind this is not all about you, it is about your spouse and your spouse's bloodline too. What if God has cut either of you off and neither of you know it? Or, what if one of you know it, but you're in denial or not telling your spouse so you both can deal with this in prayer and deliverance?

I cut off the flow of hereditary problems in the life of my child. Lord, deliver me, and my spouse so we don't pass evil foundation to our child, in Jesus' Name.

I bind every negative ancestral spirit and command it to *loose* its hold upon our child, in the Name of Jesus.

I command everything that would prevent our child from being a blessing to be totally shattered, in the Name of Jesus.

I command any power that wants to convert my child to a nuisance to be completely paralyzed, in the Name of Jesus.

I break every hereditary curse, problem and bondage upon our child, polygamous ancestors, parental addiction to alcohol, tobacco, drugs, recreational drugs, smoking, love of the world, in Jesus' Name.

Spirit of rejection, release our child.

Spirit of sexual lust, release our child.

Spirit of disobedience and *rebellion*, release our child.

Spirit of slowness, dullness, inability to read or understand, release our child, in the Name of Jesus.

Colicky or finnicky, *fickle spirit*, release our child, in Jesus' Name.

Child conceived by trauma, out of wedlock, by rape, incest, accidentally, be healed, Lord, restore our child's soul, in the Name of Jesus.

Spirit of rejection, release our child.

Spirit of unhappiness or gloom, release our child.

Lord, I bind the *spirit of hate and discord, pettiness, non-communication,* in the marriage, home, and our child, in Jesus' Name.

Spirit of abnormal fears, insomnia, night terrors, day terrors, release our child, in the Name of Jesus.

Spirit of addiction, release our child.

Spirit of forgetfulness, release our child.

Spirit of confusion, release our child.

Spirit of infirmity, release our child.

Spiritual blindness, deaf and mute spirit, release our child.

Familiar spirit, release our child.

Spirit of anger, release our child.

Spirit of daydreaming and fantasy-escapism, release our child.

Spirit of inactivity and laziness, release our child.

Spirit of indifference, apathy, release our child.

Spirit of hiding, ostrich spirit, release our child.

Spirit of witchcraft / occultism, magic, hands off our child.

I render every bad *spirit* powerless in the life of our child, in the Name of Jesus.

I bind the power and break the influence of every negative *spirit* coming against our child, in the Name of Jesus.

Any power that wants to attack our child, here we are; we are his parents, we are our child's shield, and God is our shield, buckler and fortress; leave our child alone.

Evil foundation and other evil spirits, *loose* our child from your grip, in Jesus' Name.

Father, Lord, let the Blood of Jesus cleanse the mind, emotions, imagination and will of our child, in the Name of Jesus.

Lord, fill our child with Your joy, glory, peace, love, and Spirit, in the Name of Jesus.

Let every *Herodian spirit* not be able to locate or harm our child, in the Name of Jesus.

Father, we file a divorce petition against every evil *spirit* demanding sacrifice; we are not your candidate, our child is not your candidate. Blood of Jesus, speak us out of every curse that would allow *Death, Molech, Herodian* and every other evil spirit in our lives or the life or our child, in the Name of Jesus.

Warfare *to* the Womb

Be sure you have broken every covenant with grief, death, dying, the grave, sadness, loss, and sorrow as it could be hindering conception. Those are devil covenants, and you may not have meant to form them. But lingering grief can create them. Do not think that you are honoring a lost loved one by over grieving.
https://www.youtube.com/watch?v=slw_ouEF4-0&t=4604s

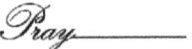

Every strange, ungodly plantation and growth in my womb, be removed now, in the Name of Jesus.

Every ungodly imperfection in my reproductive system, receive the Fire of God and correction, now, in the Name of Jesus.

Inherited spiritual contamination in my womb, or anywhere in my reproductive system, or body, be removed and healed now, in Jesus' Name.

Every medical, physical, and physiological issue, PCOS, endometriosis, tilted uterus, fibroids, ovarian issues, fallopian tube damage, PID, defects, disorders, irregular menses, infections, and **strange, nasty infections, brought on by** *spirit spouse*, polyps, et cetera, be healed, in the Name of Jesus.

Every hidden illness, be healed and my body be made whole now, in the Name of Jesus.

Every medical, physical, and physiological issue such as hormonal disorders, testicular issues and injuries, obstruction, retrograde ejaculation, varicocele, medications that lead to sterility, et cetera, be reversed and healed, now, in the Name of Jesus.

Any power that has had control of my period; your time is up, get out of my life forever, in Jesus' Name.

My womb, my reproductive *member*, jump out of evil cages and satanic, witchcraft imprisonment, in the Name of Jesus by the power in the Blood of Jesus.

I take off every garment of *barrenness*, in the Name of Jesus.

Some of the following is excerpted from my book, **Prayers Against Demonic Cobwebs,** from the chapter entitled, *Barrenness, Fibroids, Impotence*

I burn your silk; I light it up with Holy Ghost Fire. I burn your highways, your routes, I light them up with the Fire of the Holy Ghost.

Silk Trade Routes in the Spirit–, spiritual silk routes, I annihilate, I bombard you, I use the weapons from the armory of God, the treasury of His weapons and I ignite, incinerate, cut, shave, raze, destroy, disconnect, confuse, melt and zap the power of your silk routes that involve me in any way, and render them null, void, useless and ineffective, in Jesus' Mighty Name.

Forget my name, lose my location, receive Holy Ghost Smoke, Holy Ghost Fire and mass confusion now, in the Name of Jesus.

Lord, let the Blood of Jesus wash me clean of every demonic sickness, affliction, and infirmity caused by coming into contact with any demonic cobweb, in the Name of Jesus.

Mercy, Lord – I cry for Mercy –

I come against *barrenness*. Fallopian tube blockage as a result of cobweb attack, be disentangled now and my tubes become patent to work as God intended, in the Name of Jesus.

Agent of darkness who caused barrenness of any kind, in my life, receive Judgment for messing with a child of God, in Jesus' Name.

Mercy Lord, I cry Mercy –

Fibroids as a result of cobweb attack, be dissolved and expelled now, or miraculously, spiritually, surgically excised by the hand of the Great Physician, in the Name of Jesus.

Every Satanic arrow projected into my womb, return back to sender, back to sender, back to sender, sevenfold, in the mighty Name of Jesus.

Cobwebs that cause miscarriage, or delay in conception, lose your power against me immediately, in Jesus' Name.

Lord, reverse the presence and damage of fibroids in my body, in the Name of Jesus.

Cobwebs blocking my womb, or fallopian tubes, be burned to ashes and come out by Fire in Jesus' Name.

Agent of darkness who caused the fibroid(s), receive the judgment of God now for harming a child of God, in the Name of Jesus.

Impotence and/or low sperm count, as a result of cobweb attack--, let every constriction and entanglement become untangled now, in the Name of Jesus. Agent of darkness responsible for this malady – go to the Abyss. You've been found out; I declare **failed assignment**, go to the Abyss where there is no water and there is no return, in the Name of Jesus.

Any satanic web purposing to lock my womb, be neutralized now, in Jesus' Name.

Every cobweb attack to cover me with shame or to cover or block me from divine connections, destiny helpers, Godly relationships and/or Kingdom marriage, I break you with the Fire Machete of God and call for the East Wind of God to blow you into Oblivion never to be regathered, reassembled, or reconstituted against me ever again, in the Name of Jesus.

I break your three-fold cord, I break your cord within a cord, within a cord, by the Holy Fire of God, in Jesus' Name.

My womb, receive, retain and maintain your pregnancy to term, in the Name of Jesus.

Hedge of fire, Blood of Jesus surround and protect me now, in the Name of Jesus.

Battles of conception from my father's house, die, in the Name of Jesus.

Battles of pregnancy from my mother's house, die, in the Name of Jesus.

Battles of pregnancy from my father's house, die, in the Name of Jesus.

Spirit of Death, abortion, miscarriage, murder, you are commanded to depart from my womb immediately, we are not your sacrifice, in the Name of Jesus.

Every bewitchment, every curse against me, lose your power, lose your power, lose your power, lose your authority to work against me, by the Blood of Jesus.

Lose your legal standing against me, the Blood of Jesus is my defense, I am the righteousness of God in Christ Jesus; you have no power over me, in the Name of Jesus.

Warfare *In* the Womb

The Bible says that Jacob and Esau wrestled in the womb. Even if there are not twins or multiples in the womb there will be warfare. After conception pregnancy continues to be a warfare. There is a tiny embryo in there forming, multiplying cells, gestating, and depending on you to protect it from Day One. Day One is the moment of conception. Like Hannah, if you are a warrior, warring for your child, your family, your marriage, and bloodline, don't stop. There is still warfare. After all, who do you think that baby is *kicking* in the womb. **Your baby could be wrestling things unseen by us in utero.** Are babies in warfare and we are oblivious to it? Pray! Help your baby, don't just say, *Oh wow, he kicked me.* I don't think your baby is kicking *you* at all.

Molech, Herodian spirits, spirit spouse, spirit children, the devil has not certain age when he will attack a human. The devil hates all humans—even babies.

Ask God.

Pregnant women feed cravings, then the child comes out loving peaches or whatever the mother ate during pregnancy. Eat the Word of God during pregnancy. Pray daily; pray often. Invite the Holy Spirit, this way your child learns to know and crave God from conception.

Let your child's bedtime stories be Bible stories, Psalms and Proverbs. When he/she is old, they will not depart from it. If you feed your child nothing spiritually, the enemies of God will approach and without proper prayer covering may affect your fetus in negative ways. This is still warfare. You can't diss God after you get what you think you want--, a positive pregnancy test.

Demons of barren womb, demons of miscarriage, *spirit spouse*, spirit children, come out and die, in the Name of Jesus.

I plead the Blood of Jesus over my life and over my womb. My womb, open up and receive your miracle, in the Name of Jesus.

(Some of the following is from my book, **EVIL TOUCH** https://a.co/d/8mplYXb)

Illegal occupants in my womb, including witchcraft animals or synthetic children, your time is up, Come out by Fire, come out by Fire, by Fire, in the Name of Jesus.

Every power involved in any evil touch on me or my stomach, hands off! and die, die, die, in the Name of Jesus. You will not sow poverty or sorrow into my life, in the Name of Jesus.

You will not steal blessings from my life, nor virtue from me, or my child, in Jesus' Name.

My Star, arise. Shine, in the Name of Jesus. In my star is my relationships, marriage, family, children.

(Rescue, set your star free in this prayer from Warfare Prayer Channel: https://www.youtube.com/watch?v=_IKdN5LdttM&t=22687s)

Finger of witches blocking my womb, wither by Fire, in the Name of Jesus.

My stolen or exchanged womb, come back to me, in the Name of Jesus.

I drink the Blood of Jesus to heal my heart, my womb, and my life, in the Name of Jesus.

Witch's stone blocking my fallopian tubes, come out by Fire, in the Name of Jesus.

Strange fire burning in my womb, die, in the Name of Jesus.

Hands of the Almighty God, rest upon my womb and start a new thing in me, in the Name of Jesus.

Inflammation and every disorder of the womb, be healed now, by the touch of God, by the Blood of Jesus, in the Name of Jesus

Wet dream, any sex in the dream, I terminate you by the power of God in Jesus Christ.

Gynecological issues in my womb, Lord Jesus, flush them out, in the Name of Jesus.

Urological issues in my reproductive system, Lord Jesus, heal them, in Jesus' Name.

Arrow of barrenness fired against my life, go back to your owner, in Jesus' Name.

Witchcraft powers attacking my womb, Holy Ghost hailstones, bombard them to defeat, in the Name of Jesus.

Female: I take back my eggs from every evil hand, in the Name of Jesus.

Male: I recover all lost sperm from every evil seed thief. Lord, I repent of all spilled seed, and I renounce masturbation, in Jesus' Name.

My womb, be made whole, well, fertile, strong. I shall no longer be called *barren*, in the Name of Jesus.

Seed of barrenness satanically sown against my life, be removed by the Blood of Jesus.

I rebuke the *spirit of miscarriage*. I stand on the authority of the Word which says, **There shall be no one miscarrying or barren in**

your land. I will fulfill the number of your days. (Exodus 23:26)

I cast the *spirit of miscarriage* out of my life right now. Your yoke and bondage over my life is destroyed, in Jesus' Name.

Father God, I stand on the authority of Your Word. I rebuke the *spirit of barrenness* and I cast it out right now, out of my life and the life of my spouse, in Jesus' Name.

By the Power of God, I command my seed to reproduce, I command my egg to fertilize now, in Jesus' Name. (I command my seed to fertilize my wife's egg now, in the Name of Jesus.)

I receive the fruit of the womb right now, in the Name of Jesus.

I command my children to come to me, now, in Jesus' Name.

*Spirit of Herod, Spirit of Molech, any power that c*auses miscarriages, I rebuke you over my life. Every access you have had to my womb is sealed now against every access point, in Jesus' Name.

Delivery Warfare

Pray

Battles of healthy childbirth--, labor and delivery from my father's house, die, in the Name of Jesus.

Blessed we are in the fruit of the body, by the Word of God. (Deuteronomy 7:14-15).

Lord, thank You for making us plenteous in, the fruit of the body by the covenant made with our fathers. (Deuteronomy 28:4, 11)

Thank You Lord, that we shall not cast our young, nor be barren in this land and You will give us long life, in the Name of Jesus.

Lord, thank You for increasing us more and more, and our children, in the Name of Jesus. (Exodus 23:26)

Thank You for making us fruitful wives, (Ps 128:3) and for saving us in childbearing, (1Tim 2:15).

The blessings of Abraham come upon us, through Jesus Christ, in the Name of Jesus and we receive the promise of the Spirit, through faith. (Gal 3:13-14)

Lord, let your healing power flow into every area of my body relating to conception and childbearing.

Father, quicken everything concerning my conception and childbearing, in Jesus' Name.

Let every problem arising from extended labor and childbirth, be canceled before it ever happens, in the Name of Jesus.

Lord, block any evil placental manipulation after the birth of our child, in Jesus' Name.

I bind and paralyze every spiritual activity contrary to the peace of our home, pregnancy, child, and delivery, in the Name of Jesus.

I cancel all visions, dreams, words, and curses contrary to conception and childbearing, in my life, in Jesus' Name.

Let my womb receive the perfect peace of God that passes all understanding, now and through delivery, in the Name of Jesus.

Let no evil hands touch me, my life, my womb, my child, especially during gestation and delivery, in the Name of Jesus.

I command every negative imagination and word against childbearing to have no effect on me, in the Name of Jesus.

I decree that no sickness, defect, deformity or illness shall locate our child, in Jesus' Name.

I decree sound health and wholeness into the spirit, soul and body of our child, in the Name of Jesus.

Baby, I cover you with the Blood of Jesus and surround you with a hedge of Divine Fire, in the Name of Jesus.

Lord, let our child's respiratory, digestive and circulatory systems be normal, strong, and healthy, in the Name of Jesus.

Baby, hear the Word of the Lord, move into position at the right time, you will be head down at birth, in the Name of Jesus.

Umbilical cord, you will be the perfect length and position, not around our baby's neck, in the Name of Jesus.

I break every covenant of delayed or late childbearing by the Fire of the Holy Spirit and the Blood of Jesus.

Lord, let labor and delivery be efficient, safe and Godly, in the Name of Jesus.

Evil human agents, my child is not your candidate. I am not your candidate, you get out of our lives, in the Name of Jesus.

Lord, let every hand and every heart that touches me or our child in labor and delivery be of You and Your Spirit, and no other, in the Name of Jesus.

In this warfare, Lord, surround us with a wall of Fire and an angelic host for safe delivery and release from the hospital or birthing center.

Keep Praying for Your Child

Warfare for your child – **child warfare leads to child welfare.** See that your child fares well in life.

You might as well start praying for your child now because that's what you'll be doing for a lifetime. As much warfare as it takes to meet a Kingdom spouse, date, marry, conceive, gestate, and deliver, there is even more warfare once your child arrives.

I break any curse placed on our child to torment their parents. Parents: forgive everyone for the sake of peace in your marriage and home, in the Name of Jesus.

I break the curse of, Wait until you have kids spoken either in jest, or seriously by our parents when we misbehaved, ourselves, in Jesus' Name.

Lord, I pray that my spouse and I are firm, but not too strict or too lenient, as to damage our child, in Jesus' Name.

Lord, let our child live in safety, in a loving home where there is no trauma due to loss of the home due to fire, flood or other natural, or man-made disasters, in Jesus' Name.

As parents, Lord, let us walk in Wisdom and Godly maturity, not immaturity, in the Name of Jesus.

Lord, give us Divine health and stamina that we are not too old or too tired to parent, in Jesus' Name.

Lord, give us Wisdom to bring up our child in the fear and admonition of the Lord, not being afraid to discipline properly, not provoking our child to anger, in Jesus' Name.

Lord, protect our child from sexual trauma and molestation 24 hours a day, wherever they go, wherever they are, in Jesus' Name.

Lord, protect our child from spiritual and physical trauma, by evil adults, ignorant friends, and schoolmates, in Jesus' Name.

Lord, let our child be safe on the way to, from, and in daycare and school, throughout their entire education, and beyond, in the Name of Jesus.

Thank You, Lord for our healthy child born at the right time according to Your plans for our lives, and Your plan for our child's life, in Jesus' Name.

Lord, give us Wisdom to care for and nurture our child without overindulging, in the Name of Jesus.

Lord, thank You for life, Health and wellbeing so that as parents, we live and not die for the sake of Your purposes and for the sake of our child.

Lord, give us Godly, agape love as well as parental love. Lord, let our child love us and not be disrespectful or incur the Curse of dishonoring parents, in Jesus' Name.

Lord, let us not fear our children, not worship them, but train them, teach them, and bring them up in good order, in Jesus' Name.

Lord, do not let me overdo it, living through my children, or step over into their life to use it, consume it, or harm it, their purpose, or their destiny, in any way, in Jesus' Name.

Father, make me an excellent parent, like You.

Lord, I break every evil covenant and curse of idolizing or worshipping children, in the Name of Jesus.

Grow us as parents where we need to grow up, emotionally, spiritually. Make us one and make us one with You.

Lord, pave the way for our child's education, future spouse, and success. Make crooked paths straight, level the playing field and give our child divine favor and grace, in balance, without spoiling him, in Jesus' Name.

Household Witchcraft

Household witchcraft again? Yup. It won't stop unless you **make it stop**. Evil altars are set up in your house or your father's house by *household witches*. You don't have to go home to be hit with witchcraft; a witch can send up to 10 curses per hour at you. But, if you know you are hated by relatives and every time you go home and they see how well you are doing, how successful, how happy -- you get another dose of spells and curses and vexations? *Really*? Is that what you want? Household witchcraft is a Goliath, a giant, and if you don't stop it, if you don't take it down then those curses are waiting for your child.

Is your conception delay that God is seeing that you are not going to be spiritual, so He is sparing a child that life? *Ask Him.*

Regarding household witchcraft, you may not be able to think of _who_ would want to do harm to you. It may never be who you think it is. Or you could think it is someone and it is *so* not them. Yeah, you're nice and respectable to everyone, so that Golden Rule should apply, right? Nope, not with witches, even if they are relatives.

(There are more prayers against household witchcraft in the **Prayers for Barrenness, For Success in Business and Life,** *Book 1*)

Thunder of God, locate and dismantle the natural and/or spiritual throne of witchcraft in or over my household, in Jesus' Name.

Every seat of witchcraft in my household be roasted with the Fire of God, in Jesus' Name.

Thunder of God, scatter beyond redemption, the witchcraft in my household and bloodline (father's house), in Jesus' Name.

Every stronghold of household witches, be destroyed, utterly, in Jesus' Name.

I break free from every bondage of witchcraft covenant, in the Name of Jesus.

Any witchcraft coven in which any of my blessings are hidden, burn to ashes, by the Fire of God, in the Name of Jesus.

I frustrate every plot, device, scheme, and project of witchcraft designed to affect any area of my life, in the Name of Jesus.

Any organ of my body that has been exchanged for another through witchcraft manipulation, be replaced, *post haste*, in the Name of Jesus.

I resist and reverse the effect of any witchcraft invocation or summoning of my spirit or soul, in the Name of Jesus.

Household wickedness against my marriage: stand down. (X3) or receive the wrath of God.

Household witchcraft against my conception, gestation, labor, and delivery, stand down. (X3) or receive the wrath of God.

Household witchcraft against our child in any way, let your power die, in Jesus' Name.

Every incantation, incision, hex, or vex working against me be neutralized. I send all live spiritual ammo sent against me, back to sender, in Jesus' Name.

I break every curse by jealous exes, jealous friends, current and former coworkers and associates, jealous family members, jealous strangers, and enemies, in Jesus' Name.

I break every clinical and medical curse, in Jesus' Name.

I break every curse issued by satanic ministers, in the Name of Jesus.

I break every curse emanating from evil prophecies, in the Name of Jesus.

Amen.

Pregnancy Dreams

Medical doctors will explain away pregnancy dreams as fear, stress, anxiety, depression, hormones, or what have you. Doctors promote a spiritual dumbing down. We are in this world but not *of* it, so it boils down to, *Whose report will you believe?* Do you choose to be spiritual, or carnal?

Dreams about pregnancy or dreams you may have when trying to get pregnant or while you are pregnant need to be addressed, handled, and not ignored. If that means you're spiritual, then be spiritual.

Have you had a fight with a person who promised to **show you** in your waking life? One screamed at me, **You don't know who I am!** Uh, that was a real clue; those are common words of witchcraft threats.

The bolder ones will boast about what they will do to you. The sneaky ones won't, they just do it.

Bloody dreams indicate witchcraft up against you or your spouse's life. It is best not to tell everyone your business. Do not broadcast your pregnancy, especially on social media. Do not let everyone touch you, especially your tummy. Pray against evil touch, especially on your tummy/womb. This can be innocent, or more evil arrows.

Stop eating at everybody's house and whatever is brought into the office. Don't eat anything presented to you, even if you are craving.

You have broken all soul ties, yes? If miscarriage is common or pregnancies are difficult in your family, suspect evil foundation or witchcraft interference. Go for deliverance.

Nightmares may interfere with conception. Witchcraft dreams are designed for just that. Being pursued or bitten by a snake indicates household wickedness.

Seeing blood in the dream means a blood ritual or blood sacrifice is being done against you. Pray immediately. Being shot in the dream is a witchcraft arrow--. back to sender in Jesus' Name. Eating in the dream leads to defilement. Purge all evil food by the Blood of Jesus. Sex in the dream is *spirit spouse* trying to prevent you from having natural children. If your underwear is stolen in the dream that indicates that evil powers are trying to manipulate or ruin your pregnancy. Don't do nothing while thinking you just ate too many pickles before bedtime. **Pray**!

Evil persecutors. Any evil animal especially reptiles, monitoring me, every evil serpent sent my way, back to sender in Jesus' Name.

Any evil person or satanic agent monitoring me, let your power die, in the Name of Jesus.

Power of God remove all evil implantations and evil manipulation against me, in the Name of Jesus.

Every child stolen from me, by evil spiritual removal or exchange of womb, be returned by the power in the Blood of Jesus.

Every dream causing infertility in my life, die, in the Name of Jesus.

Powers manipulating my menstrual cycle, lose your power over me, in Jesus' Name.

There is much more in the video, *15 Dreams That Hinder You Getting Pregnant*, by Minister Joshua Orekhie, an expert on Biblical dream interpretation. https://www.youtube.com/watch?v=iXL-JESMLCQ

Do not dismiss an important message that God is telling you through your dreams. Be safe, keep your baby safe and healthy!

Cancel every bad dream everyday anyway, but especially if you are planning to become, or are already pregnant. https://www.youtube.com/watch?v=TKWa5-cm53Q&t=2718s from this author's *Arise & Shine* video, starting at 4:57 minutes.

Prayer for Righteous Seed

The seed of the righteous shall be blessed, mighty, delivered, and will not beg bread.

Lord, make me ready to receive Righteous Seed, in the Name of Jesus.

Lord, thank You for righteous seed and the fruit of the womb, in Jesus' Name.

Let every area of my life become too hot for any evil to inhabit, in the Name of Jesus.

I reject all evil manipulations and manipulators, in Jesus' Name.

I break the powers of the occult, witchcraft and *familiar spirits* over my life, and the life of our child, in the Name of Jesus.

Lord, I receive deliverance, and pass out any satanic deposit in my intestines, in the Name of Jesus.

By deliverance, I pass out any satanic deposit in my reproductive organs, in Jesus' Name.

By Your deliverance, I pass out every satanic deposit in my womb, in the Name of Jesus.

Every evil growth in my life, be uprooted, and cast out by the roots, in Jesus' Name.

God, who quickens the dead, quicken my womb and reproductive system, in the Name of Jesus.

In the Name of Jesus, I break every curse, chain, spell, jinx, bewitchment, witchcraft, or sorcery, cast against me.

I release myself from the hold of the *spirits* of sterility, infertility, and fear, in the Name of Jesus. All *spirits* rooted in fornication come out of my womb with all your roots, in the mighty Name of our Lord Jesus Christ.

Let a creative miracle take place in my womb and reproductive system, in Jesus' Name.

In the Name of Jesus, I renounce, break and loose myself form all demonic holds, psychic powers, and bondages of physical illness.

Spirit spouse of every kind. My body is the temple of the Holy Spirit, I am redeemed, cleansed, sanctified, and set aside, in the Name of Jesus.

All *spirits* rooted in pornography, come out of my womb, my reproductive system, my entire body, with all your roots, in the mighty Name of Jesus Christ.

I reverse every evil manipulation done against my manhood, virility, fertility, and reproductive capabilities with my sperm, blood, or other bodily fluids, in Jesus' Name.

All *spirits* rooted in or attached to sexual perversion, come out of my womb, and entire body, with all your roots, in the Mighty Name of Jesus.

I reverse every evil manipulation carried out against my womb, sexual organs, or person using my menstrual pads or period dates, in the Name of Jesus.

I reverse any known or unknown evil done against me or my womb by any medical personnel, in the Name of Jesus.

I annul every satanic marriage to my father. I annul every satanic marriage to Satan. I annul every satanic marriage to any item, thing, or animal, in the Name of Jesus.

I annul every satanic marriage to *spirit spouse*, of any variety or description, or any other evil entity, in the Name of Jesus.

All satanic networks against my being fruitful, die, in the Name of Jesus.

Blood of Jesus sanitize my womb and anoint it for the ministry of conception, gestation, delivery, and childbirth, in Jesus' Name.

I break every anti-marriage and antipregnancy curse, in the Name of Jesus.

All *spirits* connected to or traveling with *spirit spouse*, come out with all your roots, in the Name of Jesus.

All *spirits* rooted in masturbation, come out of my life, womb, and reproductive system with all your roots, in Jesus' Mighty Name.

I release myself and my entire reproductive system from every inherited deformity, in the Name of Jesus.

My womb, receive the power to conceive, retain, maintain, and deliver, in the Mighty Name of Jesus Christ.

RIGHTEOUS SEED OF THE LORD, COME FORTH, COME FORTH, IN THE NAME OF JESUS.

Children Get Along Together

A brother is born for adversity, but that doesn't mean you have to have squabbling children. Pray for peace in your home, and family. Pray that your children get along well without inordinate affection and soul ties because neither is emotionally or spiritually healthy.

Lord, give us a healthy, peaceful, Godly home, before and after children, in Jesus' Name.

Lord, bind us together as a family with *agape* and brotherly love, with no inordinate affection or favoritism, in the Name of Jesus.

Lord, let our new family member be loved and accepted into the family. Protect our little one and all of us, in the Name of Jesus.

Finances

Last I looked, it took upward of $40,000. to naturally conceive, gestate, and deliver a baby and get that baby through his or her first year of life. $40K. Prepare yourself. Prepare for your child that you will love. A baby can be fun, but it is not a plaything, spiritually or naturally speaking. A child is your ministry or part of your ministry here on Earth, just as your spouse is your ministry.

Lord, send ample finances to our marriage, home so we are not thinking about money all the time, in Jesus' Name. We choose to worship You, not money.

Lord, give prosperity in finances, health and marriage, in the Name of Jesus.

Lord, let our child be born into a home with sufficiency, and abundance, in Jesus' Name.

I have endured and won the battle; now Lord, I withdraw everything the enemy has stolen from my life, in the Name of Jesus.

Thank You Lord, for provision. Let all satanic banks with my blessings be shut down and release them, in Jesus' Name.

I terminate the appointment of all satanic bankers and managers, in the Name of Jesus.

Lord, I bind every lying, thieving, stealing demon and idol *god* in my life, in the Name of Jesus. Hands off!

I command the thunder of God to break into pieces all satanic strongrooms harboring my property. in the Name of Jesus.

I blind and paralyze every strongman; I take every strongroom by storm; I possess all my possessions, in Jesus' Name.

Hannah's Celebration

Win this war and you win not only your parenthood, not only your *sonship*, but also your **kingship** will be assured. This is a huge spiritual promotion. Win this war and you will be promoted.

Then Hannah prayed and said: "My heart rejoices in the LORD; in the LORD my horn is lifted high. My mouth boasts over my enemies, for I delight in your deliverance.

"There is no one holy like the LORD; there is no one besides you; there is no Rock like our God.

"The bows of the warriors are broken, but those who stumbled are armed with strength.

Those who were full hire themselves out for food, but those who were hungry are hungry no more. She who was barren has borne seven children, but she who has had many sons pines away.

"The LORD brings death and makes alive; he brings down to the grave and raises up.

The LORD sends poverty and wealth; he humbles and he exalts.

He raises the poor from the dust and lifts the needy from the ash heap; he seats them with princes and has them inherit a throne of honor. "For the foundations of the earth are the LORD's; on them he has set the world.

He will guard the feet of his faithful servants, but the wicked will be silenced in the place of darkness. "It is not by strength that one prevails;

Those who oppose the LORD will be broken. The Most High will thunder from heaven; the LORD will judge the ends of the earth. "He will give strength to his king and exalt the horn of his anointed."

1 Samuel 2:1-10

Hannah won. Elkanah won. Hannah went on to have Samuel and dedicated him to the Lord. Samuel was a mighty Prophet of the Lord. Hannah then went on to have five more children—quite the promotion.

Blessed is the man with his quiver full of children; they are a blessing from God.

You can win also, *son* of God.

Pray

Lord, give me my Rehoboth, the land where God has made room for us, for our marriage, ministry, children, family, victory, success, and destiny, in Jesus' Name.

I bind every retaliatory *spirit* and command all backlash against me because of these prayers to backfire, in Jesus' Name.

I seal these declarations across every age, realm, dimension, and timeline, past, present, and future, in the Mighty Name of Jesus Christ.

Amen.

Acknowledgements

Barrenness is a vast subject covering the fruit of one's labor to the fruit of the body. There are many great resources you can use to dig deeper. Some authors that I used for research and inspiration are:

Adekoya, Samel O, No More Barrenness https://a.co/d/bcrwh5s

James Akanbi, Blow Them by Thunder 3, https://a.co/d/3nO9Kju

Dr. Daniel Duval- divorcing evil *gods, etc.* https://bridemovement.com/category/prayers/

Apostle E.N. Livinus, Midnight Cry Prayer Book. https://a.co/d/2b5O4tF

Dr. Daniel Olukoya – Prayer Rain https://a.co/d/eBPmOMr

Minister Joshua Orekhie (he has many videos) - https://www.youtube.com/watch?v=Nvs7fvk0YA8

Prophetess Nonnie Roberson, None Shall Be Barren – https://a.co/d/3QwfPNu

Dr. Anthony Akerele-Mountain of Fire Virginia - https://www.youtube.com/@mountainoffirevirginia book, **Evil Spirit Spouse** https://a.co/d/g8Oqg3Y

Warfare Prayer Channel videos cited have credits https://www.youtube.com/watch?v=_IKdN5LdttM

Christian books by this author

AK: Adventures of the Agape Kid

AMONG SOME THIEVES

Ancestral Powers

As My Soul Prospers

Behave

Churchzilla (Wanna-Be Bride of Christ)

The Coco-So-So Correct Show

Demonic Cobwebs

Demonic Time Bombs

Demons Hate Questions

Do Not Orphan Your Seed

Do Not Work for Money

Don't Refuse Me Lord

Every Evil Bird

Evil Touch

The FAT Demons

Fruit of the Womb: Prayers Against Barrenness, Book 2

got Money?

Let Me Have a Dollar's Worth

Living for the NOW of God

Lord, Help My Debt

Lose My Location

Made Perfect In Love

The Man Safari *(I'm Just Looking)*

Marriage Ed., *Rules of Engagement & Marriage*

Motherboard: *Key to Soul Prosperity*

My Life As A Slave

Name Your Seed

Plantation Souls

The Poor Attitudes of Money

Power Money: Nine Times the Tithe

The Power of Wealth

Prayers Against Barrenness, For Success in Business and Life, *Book 1*

Seasons of Grief

Seasons of War

Second Marriage, Third Marriage any Marriage

SOULS in Captivity

Soul Prosperity: Your Health & Your Wealth

The *spirit* of Poverty

This Is *NOT* That: How to Keep Demons from Coming at You

The Throne of Grace, *Courtroom Prayers*

Warfare Prayer Against Poverty

When the Devourer is Rebuked

The Wilderness Romance

Other Journals & Devotionals by this author:

The Cool of the Day – Journal

got HEALING? Verses for Life

got HOPE? Verses for Life

got WISDOM? Verses for Life

got GRACE? Verses for Life

got JOY? Verses for Life

got LOVE? Verses for Life

He Hears Us, Prayer Journal

I Have A Star, Dream Journal

I Have A Star, Guided Prayer Journal,

J'ai une Etoile, Journal des Reves

Let Her Dream, Dream Journal *in colors*

Men Shall Dream, Dream Journal,

My Favorite Prayers (in 4 styles)

My Sowing Journal

Tengo una Estrella, Diario de Sueños

Illustrated children's books by Dr. Miles

Big Dog (8-book series)

Do Not Say That to Me

Every Apple

Fluff the Clouds

I Love You All Over the World

Imma Dance

The Jump Rope

Kiss the Sun

The Masked Man

Not During a Pandemic

Push the Wind

Tangled Taffy

What If?

Wiggle, Wiggle; Giggle, Giggle

Worry About Yourself

You Did Not Say Goodbye to Me

www.ingramcontent.com/pod-product-compliance
Lightning Source LLC
Chambersburg PA
CBHW070855050426
42453CB00012B/2205